Now We Enslave Ourselves

Poems of Faith and Liberation

Engelhardt Tjimbinae Ngatjikare

authorHOUSE

AuthorHouse™ UK
1663 Liberty Drive
Bloomington, IN 47403 USA
www.authorhouse.co.uk
Phone: UK TFN: 0800 0148641 (Toll Free inside the UK)
UK Local: (02) 0369 56322 (+44 20 3695 6322 from outside the UK)

© 2023 Engelhardt Tjimbinae Ngatjikare. All rights reserved.

No part of this book may be reproduced, stored in a retrieval system, or transmitted by any means without the written permission of the author.

Published by AuthorHouse 04/20/2023

ISBN: 978-1-7283-7962-3 (sc)
ISBN: 978-1-7283-7964-7 (hc)
ISBN: 978-1-7283-7963-0 (e)

Library of Congress Control Number: 2023900984

Print information available on the last page.

Any people depicted in stock imagery provided by Getty Images are models, and such images are being used for illustrative purposes only. Certain stock imagery © Getty Images.

Holy Bible, New International Version®, NIV® Copyright ©1973, 1978, 1984, 2011 by Biblica, Inc.® Used by permission. All rights reserved worldwide.

This book is printed on acid-free paper.

Because of the dynamic nature of the Internet, any web addresses or links contained in this book may have changed since publication and may no longer be valid. The views expressed in this work are solely those of the author and do not necessarily reflect the views of the publisher, and the publisher hereby disclaims any responsibility for them.

Contents

Preface xi
Acknowledgements xiii

Arise 1
The Test of Friendship 3
They Let Me Down.. 5
What Do They Gain? 7
Carry Me Now 9
I Long to Be Home... 11
The Cross I Carry Is Heavy 13
Just Stand... 15
Just Do It 17
Your Uniqueness 19
Let Them Go... 21
We Hurt, We Weep, as Jesus Christ Wept 23
You Are Great... 25
Be True to Yourself 27
Banish Fear 29
Touch Lives.. 31
Us 33

The Lie of Love	35
They Do Not Know Me	37
The Season of Obscurity	39
When Life Breaks You	41
Do Not Envy	43
Digging Deeper	45
Imagine Greatness	47
Through trial and error	49
I Will Laugh	51
These Tears Are My Tears	53
Be Separated from Them	55
Take the Hurt Away	57
Anger	59
Why Choose Me?	61
Love	63
Truth Be Told	65
Wind Gathers	67
She Is a Phenomenal Woman	69
The Battle on the Pulpit	71
Is It the Church or Christ?	73
Jump Off That Cliff!	75
Where, O Lord, Is She Found?	77
We Enslave Ourselves	79
Sweetest Rose	81
What We See in Others	83

Hearts	85
Church Is Not Church	87
You Are an African	89
I Am a Poet	91
About the Author	95

But they who wait upon the Lord will renew their strength,

they shall mount up with wings like eagles;

they shall run and not not be weary,

they shall walk and not be faint.

Isaiah 40:31 KJV

Preface

This book has been written during a time when I felt persecuted by the church, by those I call my brothers and sisters in Christ Jesus. Those whom I looked up to as saints.

It is not to discredit the church, but it has been an eye-opener for me, as I hope it will be for those who hear my voice from afar and beyond. I was around people I thought deeply loved me with the agape unconditional love of God. The church people can be fake at times!

My expectation might have been too much of others that needed the same love too, maybe wounded birds that needed healing and were ready to wound others.

Sometimes those we think embrace us with Godly love become the ones who gossip about us, even to the gallows of death.

My book is rich with the kind of inspirational poetry, rarely seen in this century, that will motivate us to arise and see beyond the storms like an eagle soaring high above the dark clouds of life.

I am encouraging us as Black people, so that we don't enslave ourselves in this Western world and its complex of modern slavery. Beware of ideologies that come forth so innocently and attractively but are snares to control and enslave humanity.

Acknowledgements

Therefore encourage one another and build one another up, just as you are doing.

1 Thessalonians 5:11 (ESV)

This verse commands Christians to encourage and lift up fellow followers of Jesus Christ, and I would like to thank those who have offered this encouragement to me.

Thank you, Elder Roselyn Apondi Ondier, for being who you are in the Lord Jesus Christ, for your encouragement as a woman of God towards my uplift as a man of God and more so to the body of Christ Jesus, and for pushing me to complete many endeavours I have embarked on, such as my studies. Your relentless sacrifices, including financially, will never be forgotten. Not that I derailed, but in your doing so I was more inspired and motivated to continue with evangelism and the winning of souls for the Kingdom of God—and in the same breath to devote my life to Christ Jesus my Lord and Saviour.

I would also like to acknowledge Mr Serdar Duman, who was at first my employer and later became my best friend and has remained so now for many years. A Muslim in religion, he has stood by my side in troubled times when those of my own Christian faith deserted me. This has taught me an unforgettable lesson: that the Lord Jesus Christ can use anyone to rescue his servants.

Elhamdulillah!

Arise

Oh closed doors,
Oh shuttered dreams,
The Lord will raise you
Like dead bones in the valley.
Surely you shall come to life.
My soul will breathe again.

Oh dead bones, arise!
Your Saviour, Jesus Christ,
Is near.
Across the waves of the oceans,
Look for mine eyes
From an angle.
See your Saviour
Upon the waves.
He is near, never late:

Always on time
To raise you out of the pit.
His mercies and grace
Are new every morning.

The Test of Friendship

Friendships tested

Not in fire and flames,

Relationships tested not in trust,

Cannot stand in winds,

Storms, and times of trials.

The beauty of a test—

So sweet and painful—

Makes it shine like gold

Or lose its rainbow colours of hope.

Standing the test

Opens our inner eyes

Beyond the shadow of doubts

With whom we stand

In season only temporaly

Not for seasons in time of need

Life is mysterious, unknown,

Till it is revealed to us

By a test of flames and fire,

An open ancient scroll:

The mystery unveiled of true friendship.

Not everyone will stand with you

Through the flames.

They Let Me Down

I held their hands in mine,
Like twin brothers on the day of birth.
I walked the journey of the cross with them
Till they reached their destination.
They let my hand go absurdly
At the edge of the cave in haste,
As if I had a contagious disease—
Left me in the wilderness and jungle on my own
To search for my path back home.
I wandered back, lost and in fear,
Stumbling and falling in thorns
Piercing my skin.
I carried my own cross.
Saints let me down.
They let me down.

What Do They Gain?

I stand to perish
At the feet
Of those who profess to love me.
'Till death do us part.'
They scream aloud for angels to hear.
They put salt in my wound instead of nursing it.
The church can be hypocritical at times.
I scream aloud in pain
To ears too deaf to hear.
At their feet I kneel,
I fall prostrate,
But still they crush me
With humiliation
As if I am not one of their own.
What do they gain in my pain?
What salvation is in my tears?
And the painful seasons
I bare
I made it through!

Carry Me Now

Carry me now,

In time of trials and tribulations.

As I stand alone

Amid tornadoes and sea waves,

My ship is sinking.

O Christ Jesus, arise

Out of your sleep!

For I am little of faith.

Seasons of turbulence are overwhelming me.

Carry me now,

Not when my voice is silent.

Like the Psalmist in the valley

Of the shadow of darkness,

Like Job forgotten and scorned

By friends,

I stand.

Carry me now.

I sit scorned by the arrogant

Who do not understand seasons

And the grace and mercies of Christ Jesus.

Carry me now.

I Long to Be Home

Miles away from home

This season of Christmas,

My best friend, my mother,

Always around—

These moments even during the chains,

Shackles on my ankles and wrist.

I am away now,

As she is ageing alone.

I have crossed oceans

By myself, not in slave ships.

The search for greener pastures;

The longing to be with my mother

In the time she needs me most;

The tears in my eyes—

Home is what I miss,

Being with her.

I am torn in two:

I desire to make it in life

In this foreign land
Till my children may join me
And their future is secured,

Then home I will rush
To be with my mother.
Time is not waiting for me!
I long to be home,
But I am torn in two.

The Cross I Carry Is Heavy

The cross I carry // Is heavy.
How did Christ Jesus
Carry His cross,
Which was indeed not His but ours?
He made it His.

How did He endure
The painful journey
To Golgotha, outside the city,
All on His own,
Awaiting the painful crucifixion?
The nails through His hands and feet,
The crown of thorns
Penetrating His skull,
The spear tearing His ribs apart,
Separating His ribs
As blood poured down
Like water on the spear,

While those He died for scorned Him—
He did not free Himself.

The cross I carry is heavy.
My Saviour's cross was heavier
Than mine.
My Saviour on the cross—
In Him I will rest my cross.

Just Stand

Stand when the unknown hits you.

Stand amid betrayal.

Stand when the world turns against you.

Just stand, even when

Your heart is broken

Into pieces.

Stand, just stand,

In the middle of the storms,

For soon you

Will have strength

To carry on

Amid your pain

And complex circumstances

No one understands.

Stand, just stand.

The Lord Jesus Christ

Will show up

In the right season.

Stand, just stand.

Just Do It

Do it. Just do it.

Wake up early.

Challenge your inner self.

It is possible

Against all odds.

Push yourself

Through the pain

Like a woman

In labour.

Life is within you;

Push it out of you

To the sunshine.

Let the life in you breathe out.

Do it. Just do it.

Refuse to lie down.

Arise and push forward.

Victory is within you.

Awaken yourself

To self-awareness.

Brain power is marvellous.

Nothing can conquer

A willing heart.

Do it. Just do it

By faith.

Your Uniqueness

Do something unique.

Do not compete:

Do something better

Than yourself,

Not better than someone else.

Embrace yourself.

Discover yourself.

Dig in your own intellect.

Do not stifle your genius.

Challenge yourself beyond measure.

Challenge yourself and no one else.

Be an independent school,

An academic in your own right.

Let the world follow you—

Never follow the world.

The world needs *you*,

The uniqueness in you.

Press it out,

That blueprint in you,

The intellectual genius in you,

Your uniqueness.

Let Them Go

Let them go.
Their season with you is over.
You have outgrown them.
If they walk out,
Do not hold onto them tight.
Release them
Like freed slaves
To wander away
From your precious destiny.
Shut the door,
And God will open another one.

With fresh air pouring in from heaven
At dawn,
Breathe in deep.
Stretch your arms
Wide open with a deep yawn
Of freedom.
The Lord will shift and alter

Your own new course.

Do not be bitter;

Be better,

For the joy of the Lord comes in the morning.

We Hurt, We Weep, as Jesus Christ Wept

We hurt, we weep,

As Jesus Christ wept.

Wounds bleeding,

We hurt, we weep

In deep pain.

Sometimes in agony

We become frustrated,

Even depressed,

Feeling deprived and lost

In the wilderness.

Alone, searching

For direction, hopeless

To get back on track,

Back to our souls and spirits,

We need wisdom

And a vision,

A light shining

Deep in the darkness,

A candlelight burning far away

That will lead
Us with love,
Not hatred,
Back on track
To our source
Of power and strength.
Yeshua HaMashiach.

You Are Great

You are greater

Than your eyesight.

You are far bigger

Than the shadow

You walk in.

Your shadow will follow you,

Fall and arise with you,

But your vision and dreams

Will pave a way for you

That will make you soar high,

Like an eagle above your troubled mountain of life.

For greatness you were born,

Not mediocrity.

You are greater than your shadow,

Far beyond your eyesight.

You are greater than you.

Be True to Yourself

Be true to yourself.

Do not doubt your inner voice

Or your intuition.

Listen to yourself,

Honour your uniqueness,

Embrace virtue

Like morning sunshine.

Let those without virtue pass you by

Like vagabonds.

Please no one.

Lend a hand.

Open a door wide for a stranger

With integrity,

Then for a friend with dishonour.

Be true to yourself.

Be you.

Banish Fear

Banish fear.

Have a purpose.

Be bold; be a dreamer.

Confront your vision.

Confront your fear.

Unshackle your chains.

You are a gift to the world.

You are a miracle unseen,

A package not opened.

You are a surprise

To yourself.

You do not know your greatness

Till you discover

The *you* in you.

You do not know yourself

Till you meet the you in you.

You need to find yourself

In your greatness.

You are more than enough for you.

The world needs you,

Your uniqueness.

Banish fear.

Touch Lives

Touch lives.
Be a legend
Of changes.
Move mountains for others.
Be greater than yourself.
Wipe others' tears away.
Comfort, embrace them
In a time of need.
Feed the hungry.
Give water to the thirsty.
This is what you are called for:
Not for your selfish self,
But for others in time of need.
Touch lives.

Us

No reverence or fear for us,
Young and old run over us.
Even yesterday's born infants
Run over us
In disrespect because of the colour of our skin.
The verdict on us?
Guilty, they declare.
No wonder this generation
Is cursed,
Not blessed.
They are proud
When they oppress.
A deep smile overwhelms them,
Feel joy when they enslave,
For the genetics
Of their ancestors
Runs in their veins.
Racism is what they live on,
Like vampires
Sucking blood from generation to generation—
It quenches their thirst for hatred.

The Lie of Love

The lie of love:
Do not tell me
You love me
Because you cannot.
It is impossible for you to love me
As I am,
To sacrifice your life
Or die for me.
Your love is limited and conditional.

His love is not conditional.
Agape love, this I can see,
In death like Christ Jesus
To the point of shedding blood,
Even beyond the dying.

Do not lie that you love me,
Because love is deep.
Love is intense;
Love is intentional.

Love shed blood
Even so on the cross of true love.

Do not lie that you love me:
Your love is selfish.
You love yourself.
Do not tell me you love me:
You love your husband,
Your wife, and children,
Not me.
For them you might sacrifice your life.

Christ died for me,
To save me;
You will not.
Do not lie that you love me.

They Do Not Know Me

They do not know me,
And thus they cannot limit me.
I am great,
I am awesome,
I am adventurous
And limitless.
You cannot control me:
I am unstoppable.
I am creative.
I am not what you think I am;
I am not what you want me to be.
I am me,
Not you.
I am myself.
I am global.
I am me,
Not you.
Be you;
I will be me.

You don't know me,

But you think I am nothing.

Do not limit me.

I am a person

Gifted and brilliant.

I will rise tomorrow

Even if I fall today.

Yes, now you see

How high I am flying!

Eagles cannot reach me;

My wings are limitless.

I can make a difference.

This is my season, beyond doubt.

I am out of the tunnel;

It shines out here.

They do not know me.

The Season of Obscurity

In the season of obscurity,

We seem forgotten

By everyone, even those close to us.

We are isolated

In anonymity.

We are hidden

In obscurity,

Hidden by the Lord

Preparing us for remarkable things and greatness.

We endure the pain,

This training is unknown to us.

The greatness hides in us

Behind closed doors and walls; like prisoners

We feel devalued undermined

And underestimated by everyone.

In this season of obscurity,

Greatness happens.

We are moulded into giants

Of faith and endurance.

With tears at night,

We press through midnight

In obscurity

Till it shines like gold

And joy comes at dawn in the morning.

From ashes to beauty,

The season's obscurity

Forces us on eagle wings;

By leap of faith,

We soar higher than eagles.

When Life Breaks You

When life breaks you,
Do not break yourself.
Cry aloud for mercies and grace.
You stand
Even amid dark tunnels and trials.
You pray through troubles' winds,
The storms of abuse.
Broken bones even scattered will heal;
Wounds will be mended.
Wounded birds will wound you.
Stand strong
Like a pillar unshaken.
Even despite your flaws,
God will take you through.
Forgive them;
Forgive yourself.
Heal yourself.
You were not weak,
But young, innocent, naive,
Fragile, and vulnerable.

Abuse is cruel;
It steals your identity,
Your self-worth.
Those who break and abuse you
Are wounded children's themselves,
In deep hurt and troubled waters and pain
We will never know.

When life would break you,
Do not break.
The world needs you;
You need to heal the world.
Yes, you: do not break
When life tries to break you.

Do Not Envy

Do not envy me,

For you do not know me,

What I went through—

This you will never envy.

I am a dreamer.

You see me shining.

Do you know what I went through?

Do not try to walk in my shoes or past footsteps;

You might not make it.

Walk with me now:

Let me hold your hand through the journey.

There are thorns, potholes, and traps of life,

But I know the way,

For I follow Christ Jesus.

Now I walk by faith and not by sight.

You are worthy—

Allow yourself to be worthy;

Through challenges find yourself worthy.

Believe what God says about you.

Take God at His word;

You are who God says you are.

Digging Deeper

Dig deeper into yourself.

Do not stop until

You find the golden

Oasis, spring of wells,

Hidden in you.

Find yourself;

Find *you* in you:

The dreams in you.

The gift that hid in you

Will find you;

That is the gift that God has given you.

Dig deeper into yourself.

Become an archaeologist of your soul.

Push yourself to the limits,

For you are limitless.

Find the treasures in you.

God has your back

Behind the scenes.

Dig deeper till you have it in sight.

Dig deeper by faith,

For underneath

Lies a water well,

A spring of life,

Waterfalls that flow

Deeper in you.

Dig, dig, and again dig

Till you find your water spring within you. Dig!

Imagine Greatness

Imagine greatness.

Do not let the adversity crumble you.

Arise above your failure;

Arise above your scars.

Failure pushes you to success.

Shake off the dust of your past.

Wipe away the tears of shame.

Nurse your wounds.

Imagine greatness

Within you.

Have the faith of a mustard seed.

Run your race with boldness;

Visualise your race

In your mind before you run it.

Think greatness; see victory.

Your greatness is in your imagination;

God speaks to you through your imagination,

So own what you imagine.

Have faith!

Faith does not make it easy;

Faith makes it possible.

Through trial and error

Through trial and error,
I rise and soar
Like an eagle
High above mountains
Unreached by foes and friends.
Alone in the high skies,
Free, I fly,
Captured only by wind and cloud,
Forgotten in my own world
Of faith and confidence
And mysteriousness.
My deepest secret
Of power I discovered,
My strength to survive—
This I gain
Through painful falls,
Falling into pits.
With mud all over me,
Sliding, slipping, and falling backwards,
Climbing out in shame

Alone into the shining light,
Mud all over me dripping like raindrops,
The abhorrent smells,
I gain victory through the laughter of foes and friends.
Boldly I arise
With tears dripping
Like blood.
I weep till raindrops fall,
And clouds gather for more rain
To wash my tears away.

Through trial and error,
I stood unshaken
In my faith in Him,
My rock, Christ Jesus,
My anchor
Of strength and hope.
Praise echoes
With heavenly songs
From angels above:
Victory through faith,
Through trial and error.

I Will Laugh

I will laugh;
I will not cry.
Tears are not meant to be shed in vain,
But in pain,
For gain.

I will laugh
Through the storms
And waves.
I will surf upon the waves of challenges
As a champion
Through the seasons.

I will laugh
In season
And out of season,
Through winter nights
Shivering in cold;
I will laugh through the scorching hot summer
Till it pours raindrops.

I will laugh

Till rivers flow in waterfall over rocks,

Clear like crystal,

Showers of life.

I will laugh!

Let me laugh for today,

For tomorrow

Is not in my hands.

These Tears Are My Tears

Do not tell me not to cry:
These tears are my tears,
And I will shed them.
I will cry and wipe
My tears.

Do not tell me not to cry:
I will weep like a baby crying
For her mother's breast.
Do not tell me that I am a man
And should not cry.
I will harbour my tears no more inside;
I will release them like prisoners
To run down the valley
Of my face
Like the river Nile.
I will not imprison myself
In anger and frustration.

These tears are my tears:

Let me cry

Myself to sleep

And wet my pillow

Not from night sweat.

These tears are my tears:

Do not tell me not to cry.

My freedom lie

Beneath my tears—

These tears are mine; let me cry.

Be Separated from Them

My skin colour is
The enemy of this era.
The Western world
Still enslaves us.
Racism is
Our everyday bread and cup of coffee,
Rooming without shame among us.
This contagious racism
In our midst—
Why do we shed tears
For our racist masters?
Why do we want to embrace
Those who are brutally against us,
Who suffocate our will to live
And our human existence?
Racism is cancerous:
White will be white,
Black will be black;
An African will be an African,
Hated in his footsteps.

Be separated and free;

Be an African,

Not a slave.

Never beg to be loved

By the slave master's great-grandchildren.

Do not befriend them;

Be separated from them and be free!

Take the Hurt Away

Take the hurt away;
Live in the purpose.
Live your dream beyond the shadows.
Look far into your destiny.
You have hopes;
You are the hope
The world is searching for.
Here you are, and discovered
You have hopes. It may seem far-fetched,
But it is near you,
If you persevere
In faith—
You are wealthier than you think.
Arise and dust yourself off.
Get out of the depressed muddy pit.
Get under the rinsing rains of hope.
Let them laugh;
Run through the storms of laughter.
You will victoriously journey through these seasons of tears.
Run your race alone.

Take the hurt away.

Embrace your Heavenly Father;

Let Him lead you through,

For He knows your weakness and strength.

Anger

Anger is healthy.
It is an art, creative,
Painting emotion with a brush,
Carving emotion like a sculpture.
Anger dusts poison off
And stands up against injustice,
For justice.
Anger does not tolerate hate and racism;
It encourages us to resist abuse,
To shake others to awareness
Of the real you.
To stand tall amid darkness,
Let anger shine in obscurity,
Push prejudice far away
From the doorstep of the soul.
Anger declares war,
That indeed we are human
And speak aloud to be recognized for what
We stand for and who we are.

Anger frees us from defeat and weakness.

It alright to be angry for injustice;

It is alright to be you.

In anger we lick our own wounds and are healed.

Why Choose Me?

Inadequate I feel,

Not enough.

Why choose me

Among many?

I run; I hide.

Still you pursue me.

Why choose a broken brush

Like me?

I am a broken vessel

With holes;

I am sinking in the oceans of despair

And depression.

Why choose me,

A broken vessel like me?

You could pick up the best.

Why choose me?

I am crushed

Like wine grapes

To pour out

After crushing—

Oh, how sweet I taste,
Like refined wine grapes
Poured out!
Why did you call me?
Why did you choose me?
Inadequate I feel,
And yet you choose me:
In my weakness
I am made strong.
My branches reach over walls;
High, I jump over walls.

Why did you choose me?
Why did you call me?
I am a broken brush;
You are the Master
Who picked me up among the thorns
To paint the walls of life with me.

The crushing awakened my spirit;
Through death a seed germinates,
The birth of life through pain.
Through affliction we grow.
Oh, the crying baby through labour pains!
The joy of a mother
After nine long months
From ashes to beauty!

LOVE

Love through the window

Of wrinkles:

The beauty of ageing,

Grey hairs,

Years that have passed by,

The clock we will not turn back,

The regrets we cannot overturn—

Peace we must embrace.

The noise of yesteryear,

The silence that now stare us in the face

As we are ageing,

Does not confine us

But makes us limitless,

Our minds powerful

Like never before.

We think deep in silence now,

Powered by thoughts.

We are in our last seasons,

We think;

Yes, it is inevitable,

The transition of seasons.
Limit yourself not
In this season.

Love through the window
Of wrinkles and grey hairs:
This is our season of grace.
Be creative; you are needed
And gifted.
Never despise transitions.
Do not lose yourselves
In your last season.
There is beauty in this season!
Make a difference.

Truth Be Told

Truth be told,
Perplexed I stand
On the mountains alone.
I tried it all,
Even to end it all;
But still I stand,
And did not jump
Off this endless curve
Into the darkest abyss
I knew not.
Light blinked far
In the distance;
I turned my back
In hope.
I tried again,
Got on track
On my prayerful knees.
Life *is* worth living,
If you turn back in faith.

The human spirit

Can push back

Against all tides

Of life

Discouragement and trials.

Do not deviate

Get back on track:

Do not be derailed.

Get out of the dark

Mountains of depression and hopelessness.

You can make it

Through these violent trails of life.

Wind Gathers

Wind gathers:
Let me sail away
In the silent oceans.
Maybe on the other
Side of the ocean
I will meet Him,
My Saviour Jesus Christ,
Walking on the water.
He might call me
To walk by faith
Towards Him like a child.
I will run toward Him,
My Saviour, and not walk
For the embrace I need,
A shoulder to lean on,
Wiping away my tears
Before the winds gather.

Oh! The Saviour's love doesn't judge
My iniquity, but wipes away my tears.

Wind gathers; let me sail away
Into the deep silent oceans
To meet my Saviour.
Winds gather; let me sail away!

SHE IS A PHENOMENAL WOMAN

Her beauty amazes me;

Her joy entangles me.

She always steals hearts—mine too—

Like oceans carrying waves to the shores,

Surfers into the deep oceans.

She is a phenomenal woman:

Virtues embrace her

Like a cloak, a mantle of righteousness.

May a double portion of Elijah the prophet

Fall upon her!

The Battle on the Pulpit

Our Saviour's Jesus Christ pulpit
Is the war zone of the saints,
The battleground of the saved ones
Where we clutch one another brutally
And tear the other's flesh
Like lions in ambush.

The battle on the pulpit
Leaves a last man standing:
The stronger one stands;
The weaker ones
Trampled mercilessly under
Buffaloes' feet.
The love of the Cross of Christ Jesus,
His blood that was shed,
Proclaims the victory on the Cross,

The Lord's sacrifice
Of His only begotten son

The battle on the pulpit
Shames Him, our Saviour Jesus Christ,
Who died for our iniquity and shame.

Is It the Church or Christ?

Is it the church or Christ
Our souls are searching for?
Oh! Loud is confusion:
My Saviour, Christ Jesus.

Is it the church or Christ
That is bleeding?
The church—His blood seems in vain.

The church is weeping
Tears of distress and fear,
Betrayal and confusion.
Did Judas Iscariot arise in our midst?

Hypocrisy embraces us
At the Cross of Golgotha,
Here where Christ Jesus
Died for our sins.

The church has derailed from the Cross,
The journey of salvation.
It seeks more to be crowded
Than soul-winning, holiness,
And repentance of souls.

Is it the church or Christ?
The church is persecuting the saints in Christ Jesus.
When our spiritual eyes are shut,
The body of Christ will vanish
In the darkest abyss of hell!

Is it the church or Christ?
The Antichrist has infiltrated the church.
The holy altars of the Cross of Christ Jesus
Are defiled, and
The virtuous garment of the Cross.
Is it the church or Christ?

Jump Off That Cliff!

Jump off the cliff!
Jump off by faith.
Stand or jump?
Stand unmoved in comfort;
Jump off at risk of success.
The fear of death
Stares you in the eyes.
The fear of no return stands
Between you and victory.
You can conquer
This curve of darkness and fear,
Though the smell of death
Is imminent;
Death stares you in the face.
Be bold: take the risk and jump!

Jump off the cliff—
Your parachute
Will open by faith.

Where, O Lord, Is She Found?

The virtuous woman:

Where, O Lord,

Is she found?

I am searching in vain

Among this generation,

And I doubt I will find her.

Where, O Lord, is she found?

Should I live a celibate life like Apostle Paul

And declare, "To live is Christ and to die is gain"?

For in Christ alone I will stand.

Where, O Lord, should your son's search for her?

We find beauties among your daughters

But none is virtuous.

Should we fall prostrate in fasting and prayers

To seek your face, sanctify ourselves

Wholly righteous unto you?

We have lost our honour;

We have lost ourselves

As men. We tear our garments,
Overwhelmed by betrayals and righteous anger.
Our tears drop
To the ground like rain.
Our crowns of manhood,
Our birthright are at risk:
Some laid theirs down
Into the hands of an unrighteous woman
In a bed defiled by broken vessels,
Losing it just as
Esau lost His birthright to Jacob.

Oh! Virtuous woman, where are you found?
Is she found in the realm of prayers and fasting,
As Christ Jesus prayed till blood dropped?
Where, O Lord of mercies and grace, is she found?
Where, oh where, is she found?

We Enslave Ourselves

As we enslave ourselves,
Look at the names we still embrace,
Gazing still at our masters' nods and approval.
Our generation inherits
The gifts of slavery,
The mediocre mindset of slavery.
We are not slaves,
But we walk now into the gallows
Of death ourselves,
The gas chambers of poverty ourselves,
Awaiting our demise with impatience.
We sell ourselves cheaply on brown plates
To our masters,
Whose thirst is to manipulate and enslave us.
The thirst of the masters' sons and daughters
Will never be quenched;
Throughout centuries
It has entwined in their DNA to enslave.
They lay upon us like vampires,
Sucking prosperity and wealth away

In exchange for poverty,

Which we embrace kindly.

A true Black legacy remains farfetched

Like the sunrise

Behind the beautiful mountains of Africa.

Only when Africa unites

Will true hopes arise!

Sweetest Rose

The sweetest rose

I find

In the midst of thorns.

The sweetest rose hides

Till I find it

Entwined in thorns—

But not wriggled

To death;

Still alive

To bloom

In the seasons of love.

The sweetest rose is amid thorns

But still fresh for love,

Planted near the valley

And rivers of life.

Christ Jesus is the water of life,

The crown of thorns He wore

Bleeding the blood of life.

The sweetest rose I find
In the midst of thorns;
The well of life
Is that sweetest rose I find.

What We See in Others

A silent day,

A moment to relax,

The calm atmosphere,

The joy in other faces—

This air is so peaceful,

The moment we embrace ourselves

In the sunshine.

The sunshine we see in others

Reflects on us.

The smiles we see in others

Enters the depth of our hearts.

Love is the most

Special gift we can share with others,

Like birds singing at dawn of morning

To wake us to a new sunshine,

A new glorious day.

Hearts

Some hearts are flesh,
Some gold;
Others diamonds.
Yours is heavenly heart
That embraces us all.
Your beauty,
Not only outwards,
Is innate,
In innermost depth,
Entwined with love.
You are a heavenly flower,
A treasure in disguise.

Church Is Not Church

Church is not church
Till Christ Jesus mixes the church
In colour through spirit and truth.
Church is not yet church
Till Christ embraces the church
With mercies and grace.

Church is not church
Till Christ Jesus is part of the church,
Spirit poured out,
Revival in our midst,
Love flowing through the church,
And all we see is Christ Jesus
On the throne,
Not human hatred.

The church becomes church
When eyes are fixed on Christ,
On Him alone—

The Cross of His torment,
The Cross of Christ redeems us.

Church is not church
Till it becomes the body of Christ Jesus.
Church, awake!
Bride of Christ,
Your Saviour is coming.

Church, without fear,
The Cross of His forgiveness
And redemption.
The church is the body of Christ
When we are all in Christ Jesus.

You Are an African

The American and the Western Blacks
Who escape the colour of their skin
By being Blacks
As if they are escaping hell
Into heaven.
They confuse heaven,
Which is hell
Among whites,
As if being Black is a curse
And being white is a blessing.
Who is bewitching you?
Who? The rat race,
Like London underground trains.
Why do you want to be white?
As long as you are Black,
The white imperial racists
Will forever segregate you
And never be your friend.
Your lighter skin
May redeem you for a season,

But outside whites closed doors
You will stand, even if you are
In front of your Black sisters and brothers.
Mixed-race and biracial
Ideologies will segregate you,
Move you away from
Your ancestral authenticity.
You are an African
At sunrise and sunset!
Your ancestors were lynched
In plantations and hanged
On the nearest trees
By imperial racist whites.
You are an African!

I Am a Poet

I am a poet:
My eyesight differs from yours.
I see far beyond the clouds;
Like an eagle I soar
Past the rainbow.
My eyesight is not limited,
Chained in the comfort zone
Of religion and faith alone
Without the deeper judgement
Of humanity.
I feel the pain:
I cry tears left behind by my ancestors.
Even if I do not worship their holy fire and gods,
I am part of their generation;
The mark and wounds have been left
On me to nurse.
Even if I choose to let go and forgive,
I choose not to forget.
The thought of their humiliation still rests on me
Like yesterday:

I can hear the sounds of screams,
The sudden silence.

I am a poet.
I will be a hypocrite
If I do not speak out
And stifle the pain they endured,
The chains that encumbered them,
Their anger left me to deal with.
The freedom I now enjoy, if partially,
Is every drop of blood and sweat
Of their hard labour
Dragging heavy iron chains
In the hands of slave masters
Which took them to their early grave.

Being free in Christ Jesus
Left me free, indeed, but does not
Make me ignorant of the price
Paid by my ancestors,
Even as Christ Jesus paid the ultimate price
For my freedom.

I am a poet:
My thoughts differ from yours.
The Saviour, Christ Jesus,

Together we embrace,

The Cross of our Saviour.

I am a poet:

My thought differs from yours.

About the Author

Engelhardt Tjimbinae Ngatjikare is an ordained evangelist and street preacher. He is a God-fearing man who risks his life for the Kingdom of God. He will enter noisy clubs and dark streets at night with one aim: to win souls—a pursuit he recommends only if you are called to nighttime ministry. As a former gang member, he has mastered the art of the night and now belongs to a gang for the glory of Jesus Christ. Engelhardt has endured many persecutions even from the body of Christ Jesus.

As a politician, he heads the portfolio of a commissar responsible for international relations in the NEFF political party in Namibia.

Some of the poems in Engelhardt's first book, *Behind the Walls*, were chosen by the Institute of African poetry to be published in an anthology of verse. One of his poems, "The Titanic", was published in the anthology *Soulfully Seeking* (2007), and another, "The Tsunami", was selected for a planned anthology *Venturing Vistas*.

In 2018 he obtained a bachelor's degree in law from Jamodha University of Zambia and is working on a master's degree in business with law from Robert Kennedy College through the University of Salford, Greater Manchester. He has been accepted into the doctoral program in business administration at Golden Gate University, San Francisco.

Engelhardt is the father of four beautiful children, one girl and three boys. He was born in Namibia as the third of six boys and four girls. He lives in the United Kingdom, a country he loves very much and calls his second home.

Printed and bound by CPI Group (UK) Ltd, Croydon, CR0 4YY